REALLY FUN

Mickey MacIntyre

ACTIVITY Book

FOR 7-9 YEAR OLDS

This book belongs to:

....

....

Contributers: Under licence from Shutterstock

ISBN 978-1-912155-07-1

DID YOU KNOW?

ALL GOLD EVER MINED WOULD FIT INTO A CUBE 25m ON A SIDE.

DID YOU KNOW?

TYPICAL SWEET SODA DRINK IN A 2L BOTTLE CONTAINS AMOUNT OF SUGAR EQUAL TO 27 CUBES.

Join the dots to reveal the delicious dessert

Find your way
through the mazes

Colour by numbers

Bring these famous landmarks to life with colour

LONDON   PARIS

Complete this
symmetrical picture

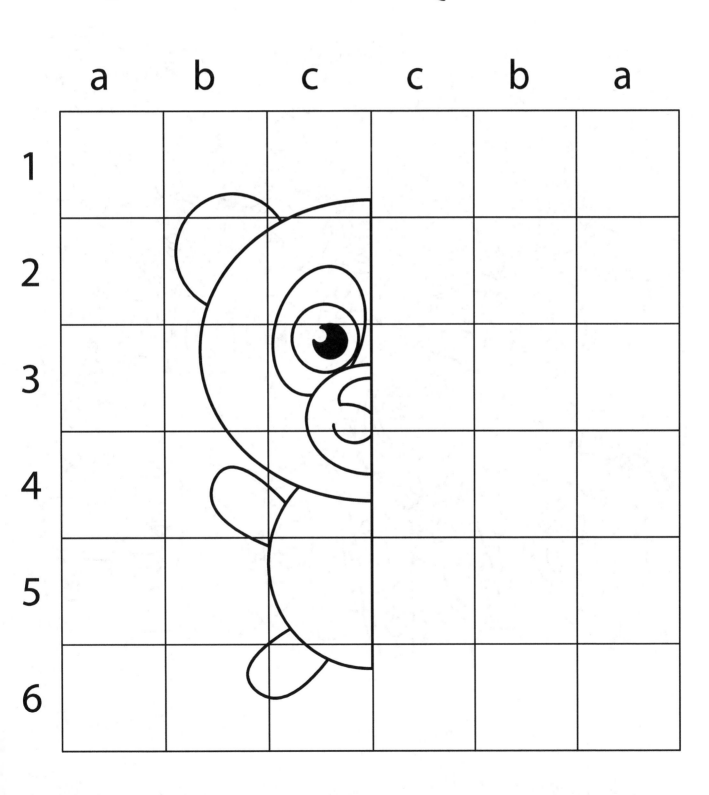

How many people can you spot?

Monkey magic

Say hello!

How many different words can you think of to say hi? Put your ideas in the speech bubbles.

Which symbol comes next in the series?

Are you a book lover?

What are your top 10 favourite books?

1.
2.
3.
4.
5.
6.
7.
8.
9.
10.

Brain tickling mazes to master

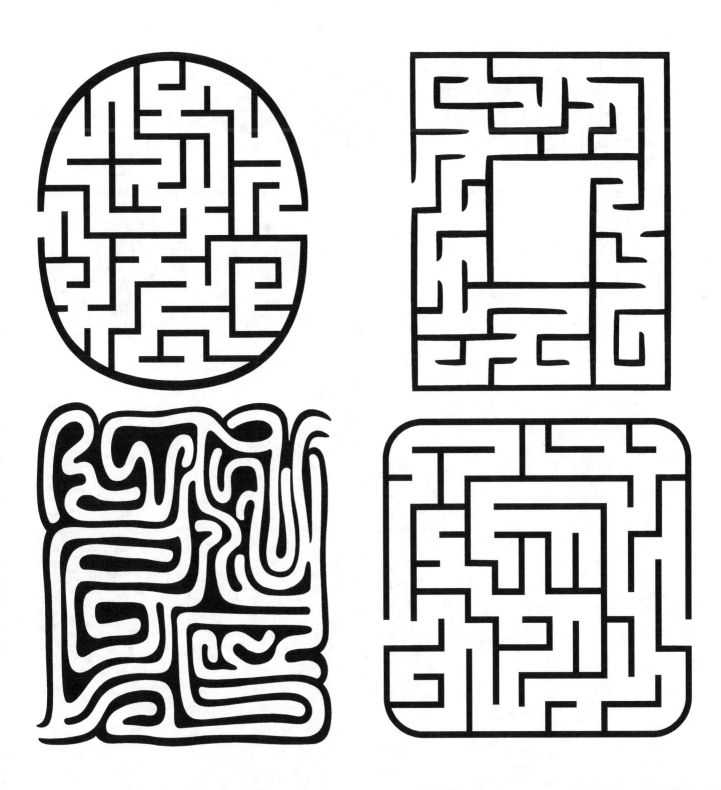

Circle the odd one out in each line

Decorate these cool pumps with your own style

One of these characters doesn't have a twin.

Can you work out which one it is?

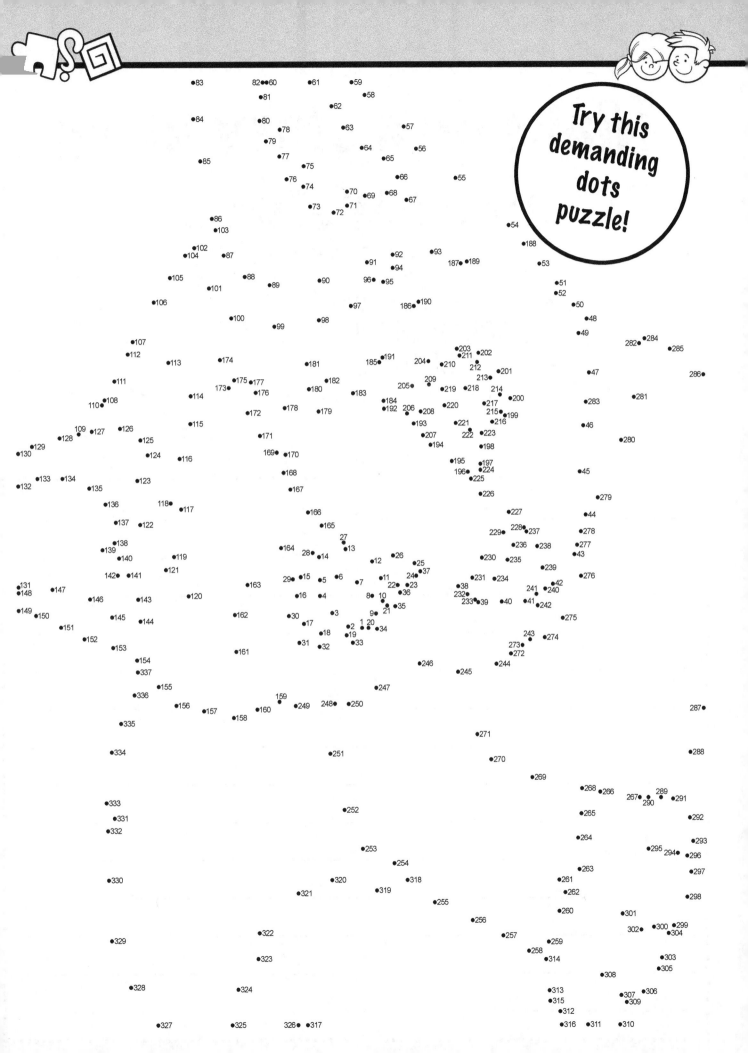

Try this demanding dots puzzle!

Make up a story using these words....

PIZZA, WOKE UP,
PARK, STOLEN, MESSY HAIR,
MESSAGE, WI-FI,
CHIPS, PILLOW, SPACE

Make a mirror image of this bat

	a	b	c	c	b	a
1						
2						
3						
4						
5						
6						

Brain bending puzzles to find your way out of

Find 6 Differences

Steal their style

Who do you admire the most? Who would you be for the day if you could steal their style. Write your idol's name in the swag sack.

More or less than?

Count the animals. Are there more than (>), less than (<) or equal to (=) the animals on the right?

5 ⚪ 4

Make these cupcakes turn all the colours of the rainbow

a b c d e

1

2

3

4

5

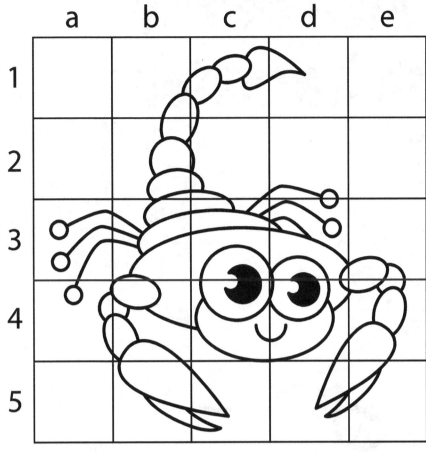

Use the grid to copy the image

a b c d e

1

2

3

4

5

Finish Harry the hamster

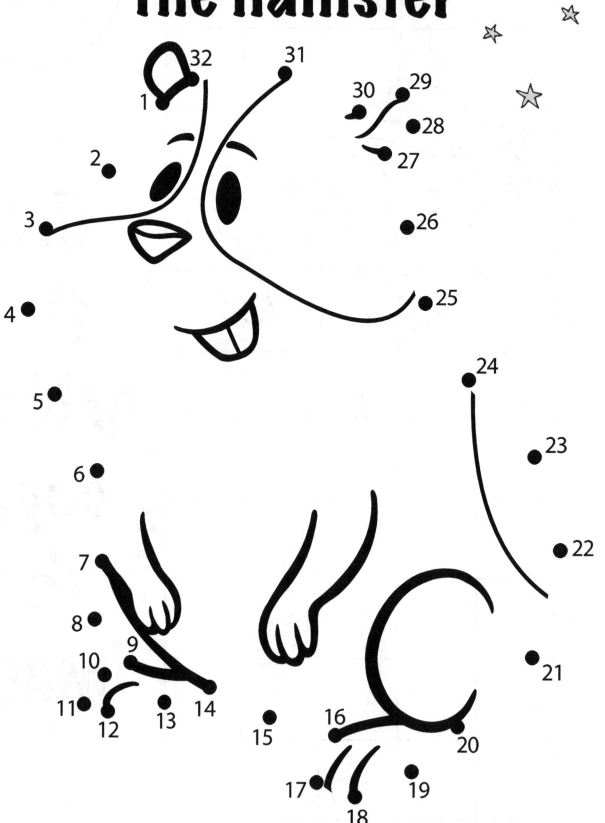

Fruit wordsearch

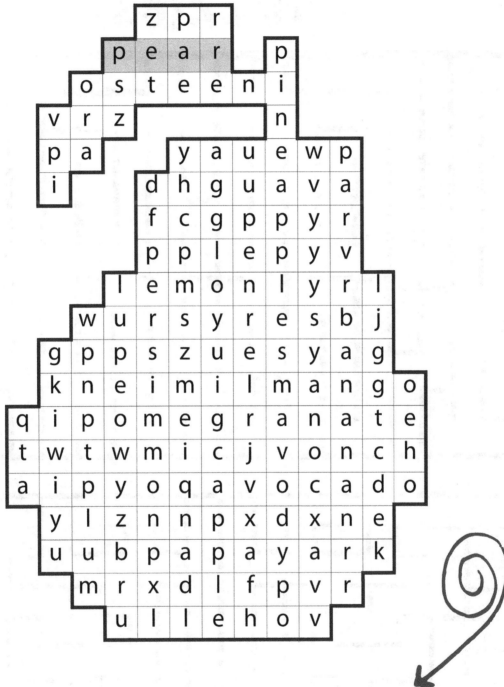

persimmon
mango
banana
kiwi

pomegranate
plum
avocado
papaya
apple

pear
pineapple
guava
lemon

Tricky labyrinth puzzles

Colour the scene

Add your own doodles

Match The Animals With Their Babies

A unicorn is born
when you complete the dots.
Add wings and a horn

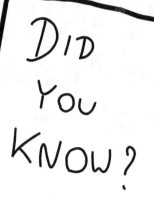

DID
YOU
KNOW?

WORLD'S TALLEST TREE IS 111m TALL, ROUGHLY 20 TIMES TALLER THAN A GIRAFFE.

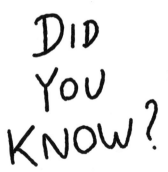

DID
YOU
KNOW?

THE BIBLE CONTAINS 3.566.480 LETTERS.

Colour the sweet treats

Dinosaur dots

50
49
48
1
17 18 47
2 3
16 19
4 14 15
13
5 12
6 20 46
11 45
7
10
21 39
9 40
8 44
22 42
23 38 41
24
43
25 37 36
26
27 34 35
28
30
29 31 33
32

Make up a story using these words....

HUNGRY, BOY, HAPPY, DIVING, SUNFLOWER, WALKING, OCEAN, BED, SWINGS, WOOLY JUMPER, POPCORN

Help the kittens to find their mittens

Colour the ocean scene

How many can you see?

Count the donuts, rock cakes, cream cakes & sponges

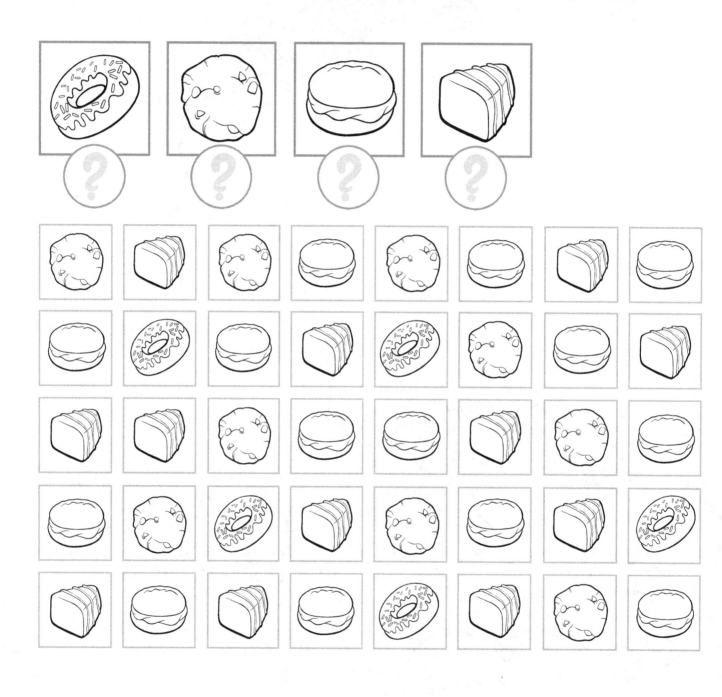

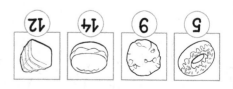

Design a donut
Turn this donut ring into a funny character

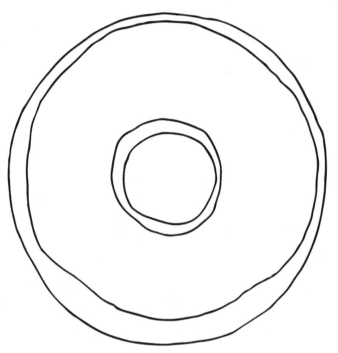

What comes next?

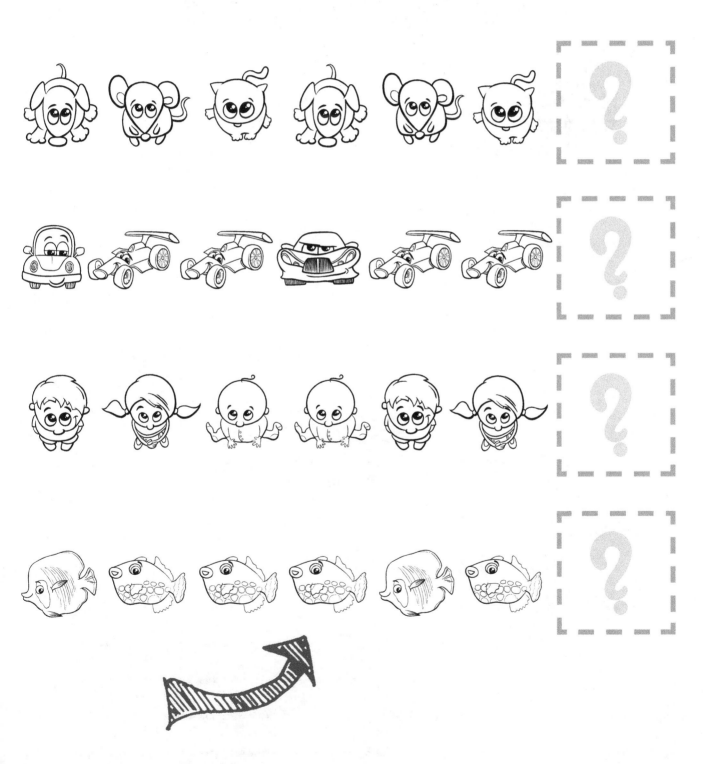

Help the puzzle piece find the way to the puzzle

Odd one out

Can you spot which creature is the odd one out?

Give each cat a crazy colour

How fast can you say these two tongue twisters?

I thought a thought.
But the thought I thought wasn't the thought I thought I thought.
If the thought I thought I thought had been the thought I thought, I wouldn't have thought so much.

****

Peter Piper picked a peck of pickled peppers.
A peck of pickled peppers Peter Piper picked.
If Peter Piper picked a peck of pickled peppers,
Where's the peck of pickled peppers Peter Piper picked?

Join the dots to complete the crab

Help the ants get out of the labyrinth

Spot 10 Differences

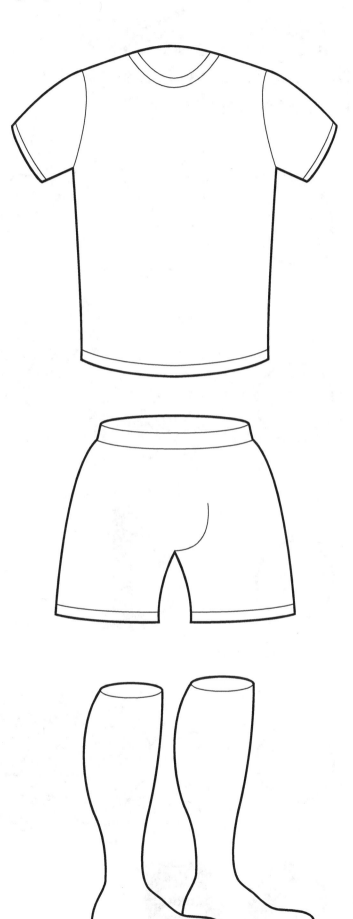

Design your fantasy football kit

More or less than?

Count the animals. Are there more than (>), less than (<) or equal to (=) the animals on the right?

Colour the lizard in tropical shades

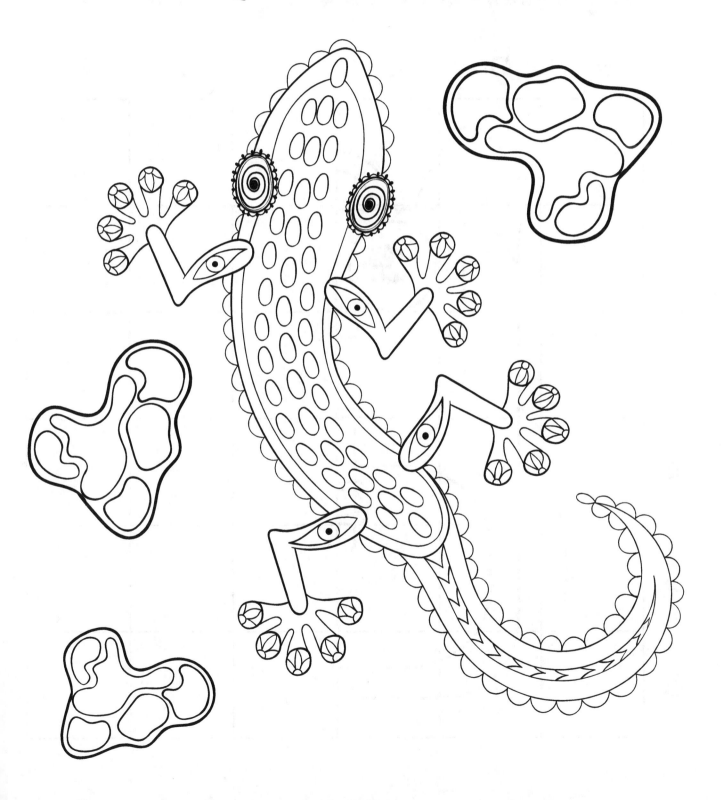

Complete this symmetrical picture

a	b	c	c	b	a

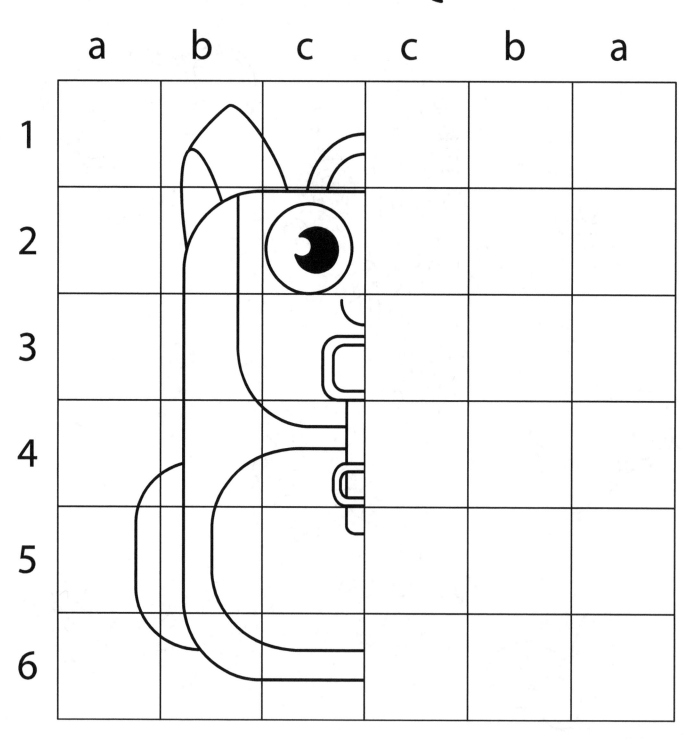

Join the dots

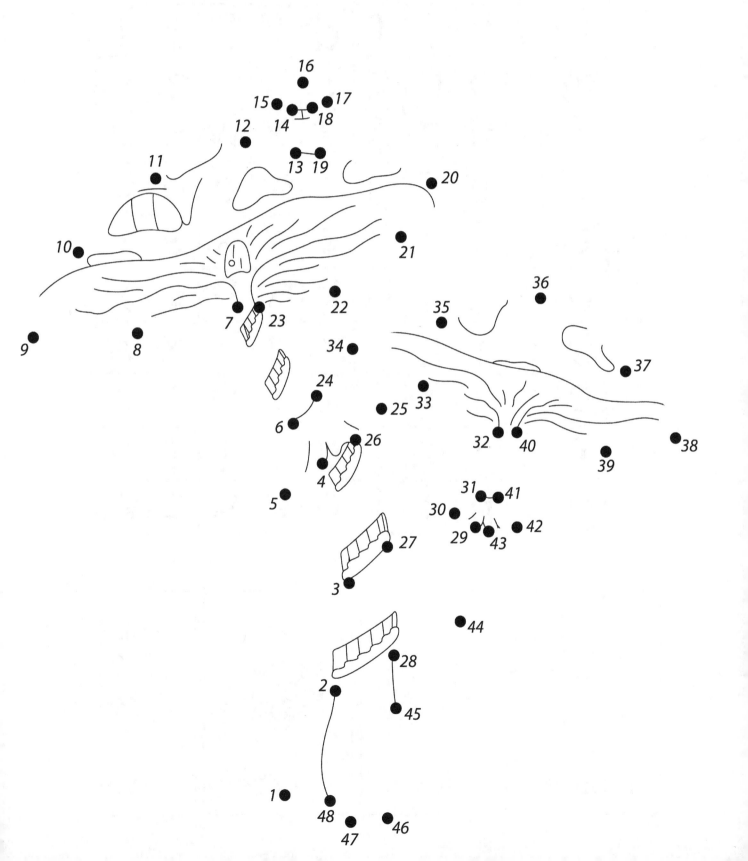

Animal wordsearch

a	w	o	l	f	d	v	h	f	i
m	n	o	p	q	r	s	t	m	v
f	h	g	z	f	y	x	w	o	u
c	b	e	g	o	l	m	o	u	p
a	i	j	m	x	z	y	x	s	t
d	b	d	j	b	k	m	p	e	y
g	f	i	k	j	m	z	y	x	w
e	d	z	y	i	l	o	p	t	x
f	h	j	m	t	u	r	t	l	e
e	e	h	j	l	o	p	q	z	w

mouse

fox

turtle

wolf

Help the spooky creatures to the pumpkin patch

Colour the angel fish

Match the creatures with their food

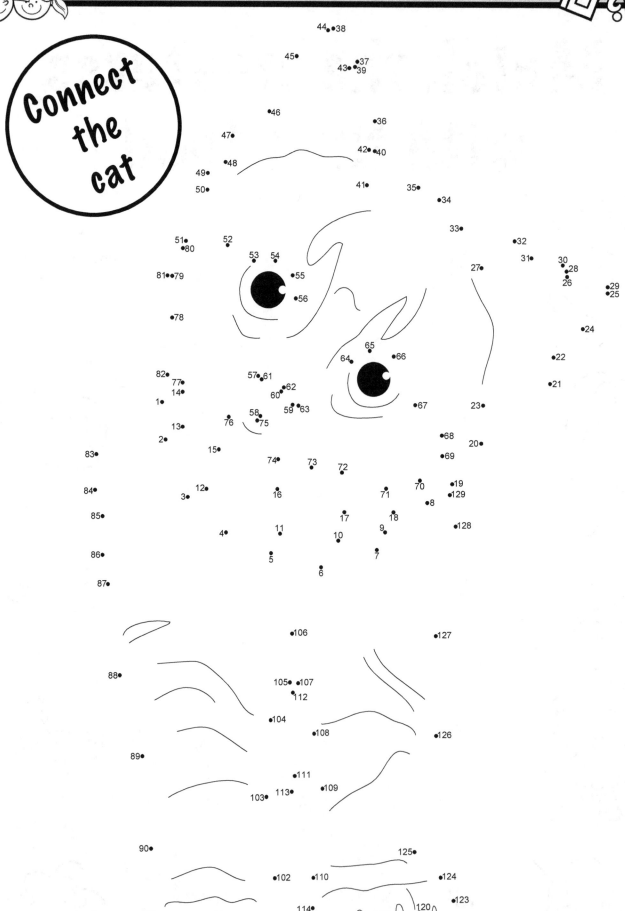

Favourite songs:

_____

_____

_____

Favourite music stars:

_____

_____

_____

Favourite albums:

_____

_____

_____

Colour the hearts

Join the dots to complete the king of the jungle

Help the ghost to get out of the maze

Colour the
lighthouse scene

How many dogs do you see?

CPSIA information can be obtained
at www.ICGtesting.com
Printed in the USA
LVHW100753191120
671786LV00010B/115

9 781912 155071